Shopping
time

Pippa Goodhart

Illustrated by Brita Granström

W
FRANKLIN WATTS
NEW YORK • LONDON • SYDNEY

Shopping time

There's lots here for young children to recognise
and talk about while they follow a little boy
and his mother on a shopping trip.
It is also a guessing game — who is the cake for?
And why buy a watering can?

Making a list of things to buy.
It's time to go shopping.

I'm riding high
in the trolley.
"Open up doors!"

"Swish!"

Sniffing hot smells of buns and bread. "Can I have one?" "Please!"

I'm choosing candles, and a cake
with icing on the top.

There are lots of books to look at, but I can't reach! "Get me down!"

Shaking and rattling!
I've got flower seeds to hold.
"Where are the
watering cans?"

Now we're waiting in the queue.

Beep, beep, goes the lady's machine.

Click in my seat belt.
Slam goes the door.
We're off home.

Mum unpacks the car.
I'm helping heave
a heavy bag.

I'm waiting and watching while Mum gets busy. "Here he is!"

"Happy birthday, Grandpa!
Guess what your present is?"

Sharing books with your child

Early Worms are a range of books for you to share with your child. Together you can look at the pictures and talk about the subject or story. Listening, looking and talking are the first vital stages in children's reading development, and lay the early foundation for good reading habits.

Talking about the pictures is the first step in involving children in the pages of a book, especially if the subject or story can be related to their own familiar world. When children can relate the matter in the book to their own experience, this can be used as a starting point for introducing new knowledge, whether it is counting, getting to know colours or finding out how other people live.

Gradually children will develop their listening and concentration skills as well as a sense of what a book is. Soon they will learn how a book works: that you turn the pages from right to left, and read the story from left to right on a double page. They start to realize that the black marks on the page have a meaning and that they relate to the pictures. Once children have grasped these basic essentials they will develop strategies for "decoding" the text such as matching words and pictures, and recognising the rhythm of the language in order to predict what comes next. Soon they will start to take on the role of an independent reader, handling and looking at books even if they can't yet read the words.

Most important of all, children should realize that books are a source of pleasure. This stems from your reading sessions which are times of mutual enjoyment and shared experience. It is then that children find the key to becoming real readers.